Put Soul in Your Bridal Shower

The African-American Bridal Shower Book

Put Soul in Your Bridal Shower

The African-American Bridal Shower Book

by

Tonya D. Evans

PICASSO

ENTERTAINMENT

CORPORATION

Visit our Website at

www.picassopublications.com

A Picasso Publications Inc. Paperback

PUT SOUL IN YOUR BRIDAL SHOWER
THE AFRICAN-AMERICAN BRIDAL SHOWER
BOOK

This edition published 2000
by Picasso Publications Inc.
Suite 904, 10080 Jasper Avenue
Edmonton, AB, Canada T5J 1V9
All rights reserved
Copyright © 2000 by Tonya D. Evans

ISBN 1-55279-039-8

Printed in Canada

This book is dedicated in loving memory
of my beloved aunt
Rachel Sirmans Jones.

TABLE OF CONTENTS

ACKNOWLEDGEMENTS

I would like to acknowledge my Creator
God, for His grace and mercy,
and for blessing me with the vision to create

Put Soul in Your Bridal Shower:
*The African-American
Bridal Shower Book*

A special thank you goes to these special people for their
outstanding support: my wonderful husband, Michael;
loving parents, Allen and Dorothy; dear sister, Wrenettia;
all of my family; and my special friends, Mary, Linda Faye,
Trivonda, Stephanie, John, Gloria, Veronica, Betty,
and Bishop and Evangelist Williams.
I love you all. Be blessed.

INTRODUCTION

Why an African-American Bridal Shower Book?

The idea for this book came into being several years ago when my effort to host a bridal shower with a cultural theme proved not to be that easy. I envisioned a shower different from traditional showers I had attended in the past. Diversity is what I had in mind. I visited several party shops, libraries, and major and specialty bookstores, and surfed the World Wide Web looking for a bridal shower book tailored to the African-American culture. After searching for months, I came to the conclusion that there was no such book in print. How could this be in the nineties, in such a culturally diverse society? Cultural awareness over the past several years has soared to higher levels than ever before. People want to know and participate in activities that reflect diversity and cultural heritage.

At that point, I decided to create some cultural games for the shower that was to take place. With little time at hand, my goal was to come up with about five games. These games were presented. Words cannot express the energy and level of excitement the ladies displayed. During and after the shower the ladies were commenting on how much they enjoyed the games. They were also inquiring about the source of the games and the theme of the shower. Instantly, I realized these ladies were eager for a unique bridal shower guide with a cultural theme that would add a touch of diversity to the occasion. With that in mind, I surveyed several ladies from various ethnic backgrounds. The one question asked was, "If you were hosting a bridal shower for an African-American woman or a woman of another ethnic group, would you want a guide to planning the bridal shower?" One hundred percent stated, "Yes."

This book offers several themes and games that one would be able to enjoy and find both exciting and educational. Girlfriends, with pleasure I have created *Put Soul in Your Bridal Shower: The African-American Bridal Shower Book.*

What is the history?

Well, girlfriends, before you have fun, let's have a quick briefing on some of the terms you will encounter in this book. I am reviewing this because every hostess may not be a "sistah," or the "sistah" that is reading this book may need to know more about the terms "girlfriend," "soul food," "African proverbs," "Kwanzaa," "pocketbook," "beauty shop," "crossing sticks," "jumping the broom" and "kente cloth."

Let's start with the word "girlfriend." The reference is plain and simple. A girlfriend is a female of any ethnic background. When the term "sistah" is used, it refers to a female but one of color, mainly an African American. Another term that is often used is "sistah-girl," which is synonymous with the term "sistah."

Let's move on to the term "soul food." What does the term "soul food" refer to? Well, "soul" is a term that is used in connection with the African-American heritage. Add the word "food" and you have African-American food. Simply stated, soul food is an African-American cuisine that can be traced back to slavery. During those times, slaves made some of their soul food cuisine from unused food from the plantation houses. There was never a time when food was wasted. Leftover food had its place. For example, stale bread was used to make bread pudding, leftover fish was used for croquettes, and so on. Some common types of soul food are ribs, liver pudding, potato pon, candied yams, sweet potato pies, fried chicken, collard greens, red beans and rice, hog maws, pig ears, liver, ham hocks, neck bones, chitlins, pig feet— and the list goes on. If you want to cook a meal that fills the air with a lingering aroma, in which the food is downright delicious, then ask the elders in your family, or anyone who loves to cook soul food meals, about their favorite recipes.

Our African ancestors were known for their wisdom (the African proverb), which was often passed down from generation to generation orally. According to Webster II Dictionary, a proverb is a short, pithy, and much-used saying that expresses a well-known truth or fact. This is true for African proverbs.

Here are a few well-known African proverbs:
• Don't count your chickens before they hatch.
• You will eat it before it eats you.

- What the family talks about in the evening, the child will talk about in the morning.
- He who learns, teaches.
- A zebra does not despise its own stripes.
- You cannot build a house for last year's summer.

What is Kwanzaa? This Swahili term refers to a seven-day African-American celebration that focuses on the various principles of cultural reaffirmation. Dr. Maulana Karenga founded this celebration in 1966. It begins December 26 and ends January 1. Each day celebrates a different principle.

Date	Swahili Term	Meaning/Focus
December 26	Umoja	Unity
December 27	Kujichagulia	Self-Determination
December 28	Ujima	Collective Work and Responsibility
December 29	Ujamaa	Cooperative Economics
December 30	Nia	Purpose
December 31	Kuumba	Creativity
January 1	Imani	Faith

The seven symbols of Kwanzaa are shown in the table below:

Item	Swahili Name	Symbolizes
Place Mat	Mkeka	History
Big Cup	Kikombe Cha Umoja	Unity
Fruits/Vegetables	Mazao	Harvest
Corn	Muhindi	One ear for each child in the family
Candleholder	Kinara	Origin
Candles (One black in center, three red on left, three green on right)	Mishumaa Saba	Seven Principles
Gifts	Zawadi	Children's good behavior during the past year

The three colors of Kwanzaa symbolize the following concepts:

Color	Symbolizes
Black	Unity
Red	Long Struggle
Green	The Future

The term "pocketbook" is synonymous with "purse," or any related item. "Beauty shop" is synonymous with "hair salon" or any establishment you would go to to get your hair groomed. "Crossing sticks" and "jumping the broom" are rituals that African ancestors performed to honor and symbolize their entrance into marriage. "Jumping the broom" is becoming very popular at African-American weddings today. Last but

not least, kente cloth, defined by Nigerian fashion designer Thony Anyiams, is hand woven, multicolored strips of royal cloth made in Ghana, Africa.

Girlfriends, I feel confident that after this briefing you are ready and we are on the same page of understanding. Now let's go to the fun stuff...

6

Planning the Perfect
Bridal Shower

There are seven simple steps to planning the perfect bridal shower:

1. Decide on the number of guests.
2. Pick a date for the shower.
3. Choose the location of the shower.
4. Create the invitation list, including addresses and phone numbers.
5. Select a theme for the shower.
6. Decide on the food selection.
7. Create a shopping list for prizes, decorations, food, catering, and so on.

When you have decided on the number of guests, secure the date and ensure the availability of the location. Now it's time to create your invitation list. You can create a guest directory similar to the one shown below.

Bridal Shower Guest Directory

Name	Address	Phone Number	Invitation Mailed RSVP	
Sistah Shower	1432 Sistah Lane, Sistah, SC 00000	(111) 555-3333	5/1/00	Yes

The bridal shower invitation should inform the guests of the following:
- who the bride-to-be is;
- theme, if any;
- day and date;
- address;
- time;
- hostess's name and number;
- RSVP, if appropriate;
- suggested gifts. Identify sizes and color preferences;
- registry information and location, if applicable.

Include directions to the shower or a phone number for guests to call if they need directions.

If you have computer savvy and have the correct software, you may design the invitations yourself. You can also design an invitation flyer. Following are some examples of flyer-style invitations. Use your imagination. Printing in color will enhance your invitation.

Soul Food Recipe

Bridal Shower

for

Summer Jones

Sunday, July 17, 2000

333 Radiance Court

Four o'clock in the afternoon

Hostess

Stephanie Bell

(222) 555-2222

Suggested gifts
soul food cookbooks, your favorite
soul food recipe, Afrocentric cooking
accessories i.e. aprons, etc.

RSVP by July 1, 2000

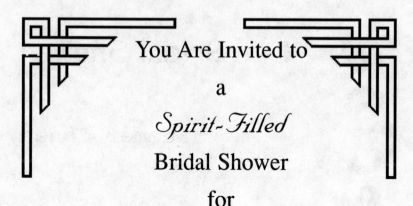

You Are Invited to

a

Spirit-Filled

Bridal Shower

for

Mary Shower

Saturday, July 5, 1999

1122 Newlywed Court
Three o'clock
Hostess
Sister Eve
(111) 555-1111

Suggested gifts

gift certificates to religious bookstores,
religious books on marriage, religious
audio and video tapes,
inspirational items.

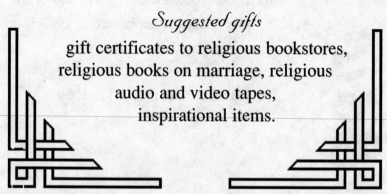

Come dressed in Afrocentric Attire

to the

Afrocentric Bridal Shower

for

Linda Faye

Saturday, July 5, 1999

1122 Newlywed Court

Three o'clock

Hostess:

Sistah Hostess

(111) 555-1111

Suggested gifts: Black art, cultural stationery, subscription to a Black magazine, gift certificate to a Black-owned restaurant or establishment, Black-produced video movies.

RSVP by June 5, 2000

Soul Food

Recipe Bridal Shower

for

Mary Cook

Friday, January 7
2233 Collard Greens Street
Two o'clock in the afternoon
Hostess: Lisa (999) 999-9999

Suggested gifts:

Soul food recipe cookbooks,
your favorite soul
food recipe,
Afrocentric cooking
accessories i.e. aprons,
etc.

Notes

Theme Showers

Now it's time for you to select a theme for the shower. This should not be a guessing game. Instead you should search for the facts about the bride-to-be. Ask her close friends and relatives about her favorite colors, favorite fragrances, favorite room in the home, religious preferences, interests, and much more.

Using the techniques mentioned above will ensure a more meaningful shower for the bride-to-be.

Soul Food Recipe Shower

Have you ever heard your mother, grandmother, or aunt say any of the following to you or other family members: "Girl, you gotta learn how to cook"? "If you want a good man or want to keep the one you've got, learning how to cook is the key." "The way to a man's heart is through his stomach." I've heard these sayings many times. The Soul Food Recipe

Shower would be ideal for the bride who
- never learned to cook;
- needs to improve her cooking;
- wants new recipes;
- loves to cook;
- doesn't own many cookbooks.

This shower will assist the bride-to-be in preparing soul foods, cultural dishes, and a whole lot more. There are no limits to what she may learn to cook.

Each guest is asked to bring a gift that would make cooking a soulful event. Suggestions: a favorite soul food cookbook, recipe cookbook, or favorite recipe. Ask each guest who brings a favorite recipe to share with the group why she likes the recipe and the source of the recipe if known. Those guests who have not mastered the art of cooking may bring cooking accessories: utensils, serving spoons, measuring cups, mitts, spatulas, pot holders, or any item that would be useful in preparing a soul food recipe or meal.

Family Roots Shower

How would you like to host a shower that would provide the bride-to-be with gifts that are priceless and truly special? The Family Roots Shower would be for close relatives of the future bride and groom. Each family member may bring a treasured gift. It may be one that has been handed down, or it may be something that the family member has made and would like to pass on to the future bride and groom.

Some examples are jewelry, pins, rings, earrings, china, crystal, recipes, pictures, furs, artwork, crafts, and handmade quilts. Guests should be asked to share the history of the gifts for the bride-to-be. These precious items will serve to keep the family history and sentimental values alive for years to come, so pass them on.

A Quilt for My Sistah

Prior to the shower, each guest is asked to select a quilt square approximately 3 1/2 inches by 5 inches. The fabric design she chooses will reflect a symbolic bond between her and the bride-to-be. For example, if the bride-to-be and one of the guests went on a vacation to Africa together, her square may be the kente design. The hostess sets a deadline for all squares to be completed, retrieves them before the shower, and has them professionally sewn together into a quilt. The quilt is presented to the bride-to-be at the shower. Guests are asked to share the significance of each square. Note: A guest may select more than one quilt square to submit. Remember that each square has a significant experience or meaning.

Afrocentric Shower

If you would like to host a shower that is centered on the African-American culture, then the Afrocentric Shower is the theme shower to select. On the shower invitation, ask the guests to come dressed in African attire. You may have cultural foods for refreshments and even a cake made using the kente design. Suggested gifts for this type of shower:
- Black art;
- Black magazine subscriptions;

- gift certificate to Black-owned restaurant or establishment;
- Afrocentric stationery;
- books by African-American authors;
- African loungewear or lingerie;
- tickets to Black art galleries;
- African clothing;
- African-American-produced movie videos;

Money Broom Shower

You can sweep the bride-to-be off her feet by hosting a Money Broom Shower.

Each guest is asked to bring a monetary gift to the shower. Upon arrival, each guest will place her gift in a special envelope and place her name on it. The hostess will collect the envelopes and clip them to a beautifully decorated cinnamon broom. When it is time to open her gifts, the bride-to-be is presented with the money broom.

Inspirational Shower

At the Inspirational Shower, the bride-to-be would receive gifts that would be an inspiration to her marriage. Suggested gifts are

- books on marriage;
- tickets to a Christian marriage conference;
- religious books, video and audio tapes on marriage.

Note: The bride-to-be may have her registry at a Christian bookstore.

My Sistah's Pantry

At this shower, guests are to bring items that are placed in a pantry. This shower would be perfect for a young bride who just moved into a new home. Gift suggestions are nonperishable food items, a carving board, a can opener, a mixer, a salad bowl, a food processor, measuring cups, and gourmet kitchen appliances.

Lingerie Shower

Guests bring lingerie for the bride-to-be. You would list the following on the invitation: size, favorite colors, and, most importantly, her taste. Suggested gifts are teddies, robes, gowns, slippers, panties, and bras.

Smell Good Shower

It's simple! At the Smell Good Shower guests bring items that smell good. Encourage them to use their creativity. Suggested gifts are scented soaps, scented lotions, perfume, bubble bath, sachets, scented oil, fragrant powder, scented candles, roses, and potpourri.

Honeymoon Shower

Find out where the couple is going on the honeymoon and ask guests to bring items the newlyweds may need or use for their trip.

Basket Shower

Ask each guest to bring a decorative basket filled with items for the bride-to-be. The basket should have a theme. Instruct guests to write the theme of the basket on a slip of paper and place it in the basket. Some theme ideas are food, bathroom, fragrance, Black movie, going away, fruit, pamper me, towels, books, inspirational, candles, and so on.

Bed & Bath Shower

Guests are to bring items that can be used in the bedroom or bathroom. The bride-to-be provides the hostess with her color scheme, and this information is listed on the invitation.

Traditional Shower

This shower does not have a particular theme. Quite often a bridal registry is set up at a specific store and gifts are purchased from the list.

Sistah Night Out

Guests are to meet at a nice restaurant for dinner, and afterwards they will go to a nice movie or play. Guests are to pitch in to pay for the bride-to-be's dinner and any costs involved in any other activities. This is an excellent activity when you have four ladies or fewer getting together.

Sistah We Had the Best
of Times Shower

At this shower, guests will have the opportunity to reflect on the most precious memories they share with the bride-to-be. They are encouraged to bring a gift that reflects the precious moments in time spent with each other.

For example if the special time was spent together at a special restaurant, then I would recommend a gift certificate to that restaurant.

If they went on a trip together and took a nice photo

together, have the photo matted into a beautiful frame.

If the movies is where a lot of time was spent, consider movie passes.

If shopping was the thing you did together, consider a gift certificate to her favorite store.

When the guests present their gifts, ask them to tell their stories of the best of times with the bride-to-be.

Take the time to reflect on those precious memories.

Set The Scene, Sistah,
Set The Scene

At this shower, guests are to bring gifts that are centered on planning an imaginary romantic evening. On the invitation, you would set the scene with fewer than five sentences. Instruct the guests to explain how they would plan for this romantic evening and to bring the items to help make it a reality.

Choose from one of the scenes listed below, or make up your own and list it on the invitation.

Scene 1:
Tomorrow your husband will return home from a business trip he has been on for four days. You both cannot wait to be reunited. You are thinking of different things you can do for a romantic evening.

Scene 2:
It's Friday night and the kids have gone to their grandparents' home.

Scene 3:
You have been daydreaming about your spouse all day long, and you want to do something special for him because he has been the perfect husband.

Scene 4:
Your husband has been out to sea for six months. His ship will sail in tomorrow.

Scene 5:
You want to have a romantic evening with your husband for no specific reason... just because.

At the shower, when it is time for the bride-to-be to be presented with her gifts, the facilitator will recite the scene that was listed on the invitation. Each guest is asked to set the scene and present the gifts to help accomplish this "Black love" evening. You will need a recorder to record the suggestions and give them to the bride-to-be.

Examples:
Guest: Hello, girlfriends, my name is Tonya, and I would set the scene by having a candlelit dinner with soft music playing in the background.
To help make this possible, here is a bottle of wine, a pair of wineglasses, two candles with candleholder, and a jazz CD.
Guest: Hello, girlfriends, my name is Wrenettia, and I would set the scene by going out to dinner at a nice restaurant.
To help make this possible, here is a gift certificate to a nice restaurant.

Guest: Hello, girlfriends, my name is Linda, and I would set the scene by having rose petals leading up the steps going to the bedroom, and in the bedroom there would be scented candles burning and love songs playing.

To help make this possible, here is a gift certificate to a florist to purchase the rose petals, scented candles, a candle-holder, tape of love songs, and a box of chocolate-dipped strawberries.

Set the scene, girlfriends—set the SCENE...

Spirit-Filled Shower

This shower would be perfect for the hostess who believes the bride-to-be would enjoy a religious, spirit-filled shower. The hostess would invite a guest speaker to come and speak on topics such as "Having A Spirit-Filled Marriage." The speaker may be the bride-to-be's pastor's wife or a female that provides religious counseling on the subject of marriage. Biblical scriptures are shared and discussed with the group as a point of reference. This is a blessing for the bride-to-be and for single women as well. Suggested gifts are:

- gift certificate to a Christian bookstore;
- verses for daily readings;
- religious reading material on marriage;
- video and audio tapes on marriage;
- photo album with religious scripture engraved;
- group plaque (shown below).

Sistah Tonya,
May GOD Bless You As You Jump The Broom
We Love You
GOD Church in Christ
Usher Board Number 1

Black Art Shower

This theme shower would be ideal for the bride-to-be who loves Black art or who is going to move into a new home, condo, or apartment. Suggested gifts are Black art paintings, sculptures, figurines, and so on.

Designer Shower

This shower is perfect for the bride-to-be who loves designer items or has a particular line of designer items she likes. Prior to the shower, the hostess is to find out what the bride-to-be likes. Guests are encouraged to bring items such as designer perfume, slippers, purses, and so on.

My Sistah Loves Books

This shower is ideal for the bride-to-be who loves reading books. The hostess is to find out the bride-to-be's favorite authors and list them on the invitation.

Crystal Shower

At this shower, guests are encouraged to bring gifts made of crystal.

Picture Frame Shower

Guests are to bring beautiful picture frames to the shower.

Stock the Kitchen, Girlfriend

This shower is perfect for the bride-to-be who is moving into a new home. Guests would bring grocery items or gift certificates from grocery stores, meat markets, and farmers markets; kitchen accessories; and appliances.

Notes

_____

_____

_____

_____

_____

_____

_____

_____

_____

_____

_____

_____

_____

_____

_____

_____

_____

_____

_____

Bridal Shower Games

Soul Food Scrabble

This game tests your knowledge of soul foods. The letters in each word have been scrambled. The goal is to see which participant, within ten minutes or less, can correctly unscramble the most words from the list below.

1. igp tefe
2. xo aitl
3. dlalocr sneerg
4. tlinshci
5. krao
6. mah ockhs
7. hicnekc nad gnislpumd
8. nekc bosen
9. rpnitu esnegr
10. asqshu
11. masy
12. wetes tatopo
13. crno raebd
14. lcbka yeed sape
15. fierd ckinehc

16. readb pudgnid
17. cbraebue ibrs
18. rpko shpoc
19. attopo alads
20. agebacb
21. almi aesnb
22. alpfsajkc
23. erd nbsea
24. sabcr
25. caehp blrebco
26. pirhsm
27. tacshif
28. nolemretaw
29. tirgs
30. ridyt ceir

The Answer Key is on the next page.

Soul Food Scrabble Answer Key

1. pig feet
2. ox tail
3. collard greens
4. chitlins
5. okra
6. ham hocks
7. chicken and dumplings
8. neck bones
9. turnip greens
10. squash
11. yams
12. sweet potato
13. corn bread
14. black eyed peas
15. fried chicken
16. bread pudding
17. barbecue ribs
18. pork chops
19. potato salad
20. cabbage
21. lima beans
22. flapjacks
23. red beans
24. crabs
25. peach cobbler
26. shrimps
27. catfish
28. watermelon
29. grits
30. dirty rice

What Ya' Cookin', My Sistah?

 If you want to see which sistah really knows what's cookin', this is the activity to play. Recite to participants the ingredients from the list below needed to make a soul food dish, dessert, or entrée. The goal is for the participants to identify what's cookin'. If they know what's cookin', they must raise their hand and say, "I know what ya cookin', my sistah." The facilitator will acknowledge the first person who responds by saying, "What am I cookin'?" The participant recites the answer. If the answer is correct, the participant will receive a point, which is recorded on a sheet of paper by a scorekeeper. The person with the highest score wins the game.

Answers in Bold

A hen, salt, milk, egg, egg yolk, shortening, flour
Chicken and Dumplings

Ground beef, onion, bell pepper, eggs, milk, crackers, ketchup
Meat Loaf

Pig feet, pig ears, pig tails, cider vinegar, onion, onion soup mix, red pepper
Pork Stew

Greens, smoked turkey necks, salt, pepper, bacon, water
Collard Greens

Oil, sweet potatoes, sugar, nutmeg, butter or margarine
Yams

Cabbage, bacon, butter, salt
Fried Cabbage

Cornmeal, baking powder, baking soda, salt, buttermilk, egg, shortening
Corn Bread

All-purpose flour, baking powder, salt, shortening, buttermilk
Buttermilk Biscuits

Peaches, butter or margarine, sugar, vanilla flavor, cinnamon, brown sugar, dough
Peach Cobbler

Butter or margarine, eggs, sugar, flour, baking soda, sour cream, vanilla flavoring
Sour Cream Cake

Butter, eggs, sugar, flour, nuts, cocoa, vanilla flavoring, salt
Brownies

Egg yolks, sugar, syrup,vanilla flavoring, butter, pecans, egg whites, salt, pie crust
Pecan Pie

Leftover bread, milk, eggs, sugar, raisins, vanilla flavoring, butter
Bread Pudding

Cheese, milk, butter, salt, pepper, macaroni
Macaroni and Cheese

Salt, ham hocks
Ham Hocks

Water, celery, onions, bay leaves, garlic, vinegar, salt, pepper, hog intestines
Chiterlins

Chicken gizzards, chicken livers, onions, rice, salt, pepper, parsley, garlic, ground beef
Dirty Rice

Celery, salt, pepper, onion, vinegar, water, pig feet
Pig Feet

Rice, salt, pepper, garlic, celery, onions, oil, ham,
smoked sausages, shrimp
Jambalaya

Salt, pepper, garlic, smoked sausage, ham, onion, water,
kidney beans, rice
Red Beans and Rice

Egg, sugar, butter, flour, bananas, salt, buttermilk,
soda, vanilla, nuts
Banana Nut Bread

Boiled egg, celery, onion, pepper, potatoes,
sweet pickle relish, mayonnaise
Potato Salad

Yellow cornmeal, flour, salt, pepper, okra, oil
Fried Okra

Egg, milk, onion, butter, garlic salt, yam
Fufu

Hen, onion, celery, salt, pepper, butter, egg, water,
milk, meal
Dressing

My Pocketbook

Before you begin this game, you must give each participant a lunch bag.

Ask your guests to get their pocketbooks, because they will need them for this fun-filled game.

Most women have a few items that they would not leave home without, such as a comb, a brush, makeup, lipstick, and much more. The facilitator will recite the names of items the guests may have in their pocketbooks. If a participant has the item called, she must remove the item and place it in the bag that was provided. The sistah with the most items in the bag wins the game. The winner must share with the group the items by removing them from the bag and naming them.

Note: There are one-point items and five-point items.

One-Point Items

lipstick, mirror, lip liner, address/phone book, comb, pictures, nail clipper, keys, powder, sponge, makeup, beeper, brush, highlighter, phone, pen, wallet, pencil, lotion, perfume, gum, nail file, bobby pin, sanitary pad, Aspirins, vitamins, calculator, battery, daytimer, peppermints, nail glue, press-on nails, tissue, candy, change purse, business card, mouthwash, Wite-Out, eye rinse

Five-Point Items

dental floss, book, Bible, toothbrush, toothpaste, hairspray, oil, spritz, stamps, safety pin, Band-Aid, sewing kit, hair bonding glue, curling iron, recipes, screwdriver kit, salt, pepper, hot sauce

The Kwanzaa Word Game

This game tests the participants' knowledge of Kwanzaa terms and their meanings. Participants are given three minutes to match the term with the correct meaning. The person with the most correct answers wins the game.

Term	Meaning
Umoja	Unity
Kujichagulia	Self-Determination
Ujima	Collective Work and Responsibility
Ujamaa	Cooperative Economics
Nia	Purpose
Kuumba	Creativity
Imani	Faith

Afro Wedding Trivia

Here is how you might introduce this game: "Welcome to Afro Wedding Trivia! This game is centered on bridal questions. Here are the rules."

The facilitator will say a word or phrase. The participant must raise her hand, be acknowledged, and give the correct answer in the form of a question.

For example: The facilitator would recite the word "veil." The participant would respond, "What is the name of the headpiece the bride wears during the wedding ceremony?"

When the participant correctly responds in the form of a question, she will receive a point that is marked by her name by the facilitator or scorekeeper. At the end of the game, the participant with the highest score wins the game.

Note: Participants' answers may vary some.

Facilitator	**Participant's Answer**
Jumping the broom	What does the bride do at an Afrocentric theme wedding?
Crossing sticks	What is the cultural activity Africans did to symbolize their marriage?
Crops, a mat, a calendar, seven candles, ears of corn, gifts, and a unity cup	What are the seven symbols that represent Kwanzaa?
Umoja, Kujichagulia, Ujima, Ujamaa, Nia, Kuumba, Imani	What are the seven principles of Kwanzaa?
Cattle	What is the animal in Africa that the groom brings to the bride's family?
Popular type of African fabric	What is kente cloth?
Imani	What is the Kwanzaa word for "faith"?
This Kwanzaa term means "unity."	What is Umoja?

PUT SOUL IN YOUR BRIDAL SHOWER

Fulfilling, eat it at the reception	What is the wedding cake?
Diamond	What is a girl's best friend?
Bride's mom's name	Who is the mother of the bride?
February 13	What is Black Love Day?
Pastor	Who is the person that marries the bride and groom?
Bride and groom toast with this	What is champagne?
Bride's father's name	Who is the father of the bride?
Bouquet	What is the name of the nosegay the bride carries down the aisle?
Ring	What is the symbol of marriage?
Bride's name	What is the name of the bride-to-be?
Fathers do this at the wedding	What is giving your daughter away?
Does not pour rain	What is a bridal shower?

Rites of passage	What is it called in Africa when the older females initiate the bride-to-be?
In some African-American weddings, this part of the ceremony is where the couple jumps the broom	What happens when the minister pronounces the couple man and wife?
First Dance	What is it called when the father dances with the new bride at the reception?
Bride's in-laws	What is the groom's side of the family called?
Bride's birthday	When is the bride's birthday?
Manages the expenses of a wedding	What is a budget?
February 14	When is Valentine's Day?
White	What is the traditional color of the bride's wedding dress?
Get married	What do two people do when they fall deeply in love with each other?
Rice	What is the food that is tossed as the bride and groom depart the ceremony location?

Wedding Brainteasers

JUMPING BROOM	YOU LOVE ME
LEFT.........LOVE	MARRIAG
THE MARRIAGE	LA MOTHER W

Wedding Brainteasers Answers

Jumping over broom   Love between you and me
Love is right   Endless marriage
The beginning of marriage   Mother-in-law

Hello, Girlfriends

This introduction game is played at the beginning of the shower. As each guest arrives, she is given a piece of paper and something to write with. Each guest is to write the word "girlfriend" down the left-hand side of the paper vertically. For each letter in the word "girlfriend," the guests are to think of a word that best describes themselves and record the information on the paper. Once everyone is done, the introductions will begin.

Each guest is to say "Hello, Girlfriends, my name is _____ and I am…"

Example:

G iving
I nspiring
R ealistic
L ikeable
F riendly
R obust
I ndependent
E xciting
N osey
D etermined

Sentimental Sistah Game

This game is bound to stir up some emotions in the room. Participants will have the opportunity to express, in one minute or less, their sentimental experiences with the bride-to-be. Things that can be shared are how you met, some things about the special friendship you share, fun and exciting memories.

Make sure you have plenty of tissue for those weepy eyes.

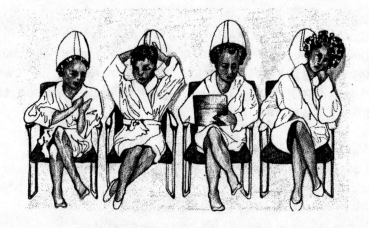

Beauty Shop Time

In this game, each participant is to imagine she is at the beauty shop preparing to get her hair done. She has encountered a problem: She doesn't know what style she likes. Within three minutes, guests are to record on a piece of paper provided by the facilitator the various hairstyles they can get. When time is up, the winner with the most hairstyles is to share her list with the group. The facilitator may ask for volunteers to share other styles not mentioned by the winner.

Some hairstyle examples are:

Bob	Short cut	Natural
Banana peel	Braids	Spiral
Wrap	Afro/Bush	French roll
Asymmetrical	Shreds	Twists
Upsweep	Ponytail	Jerry curl
Candy curl	Sistah curl	Scrunches
Plaits	Waves	Pin curls
Fan ponytail	Pineapple	Wig

 # African Proverbs

Each participant is given a list of incomplete African proverbs. They are to complete as many proverbs as they can within five minutes. The participant with the most correct proverbs wins the game. The answers are underlined.

Mothers-in-law are hard of <u>hearing</u>.
Let your love be like the misty <u>rain</u>, coming softly but flooding the river.
Marriage is not a fast <u>knot</u>, but a slipknot.
When one is in <u>love</u>, a cliff becomes a meadow.
The <u>teeth</u> are smiling, but is the heart?

My Sistah's Pantry

Within ten minutes, participants are to list items the bride-to-be will need for her pantry. When the time is up, participants will share their lists. The person with the most items listed wins the game. At the end of the game, the bride-to-be is presented with the list of all participants for ideas on stocking her pantry. The suggested form is on the next page.

Dear Sistah,

Listed below are items that are a must for your pantry.

Love,

Sistah Wedding (Participant's Name)

1.	16.
2	17.
3.	18.
4.	19.
5.	20.
6.	21.
7.	22.
8.	23.
9.	24.
10.	25.
11.	26.
12.	27.
13.	28.
14.	29.
15.	30.

Rhythm & Blues Bridal Game

This game tests your knowledge of rhythm and blues wedding favorites. The facilitator of the game will distribute a copy of the Recording Artists List, which could be used as an answer sheet. The facilitator will give the title of an R&B song. The participant must raise her hand, be acknowledged, then give the name of the R&B recording artist for the song mentioned. If the answer is correct, the participant will give her name to the scorekeeper, who will keep a record of the points earned. There are a total of twenty-one artists and thirty song titles; therefore, an artist's name may be given more than once during the game (a different song title must be given). The individual with the most points wins the game.

Title	Recording Artists
You and I	Stevie Wonder
Three Times a Lady	The Commodores
The First Time Ever I Saw Your Face	Roberta Flack
You Send Me	Sam Cooke
The Closer I Get to You	Roberta Flack and Donny Hathaway
When We Get Married	Larry Graham
Let's Chill	Guy
The Lady in My Life	Michael Jackson
Best Thing That Ever Happened to Me	Gladys Knight and the Pips
Down the Aisle	Pattie LaBelle and the Blue Belles
Ribbon in the Sky	Stevie Wonder
We're in This Love Together	Al Jarreau
You Bring Me Joy	Anita Baker

PUT SOUL IN YOUR BRIDAL SHOWER

Forever Mine	O'Jays
We're Going All the Way	Jeffrey Osborne
The Wedding Song	Smokey Robinson
Endless Love	Diana Ross and Lionel Richie
When a Man Loves a Woman	Percy Sledge
Shower Me with Your Love	Surface
Forever, for Always, for Love	Luther Vandross
For Always	BeBe and CeCe Winans
You Are the Sunshine of My Life	Stevie Wonder
One in a Million	Larry Graham
You Are My Heaven	Roberta Flack and Donny Hathaway
One Day I Will Marry You	Michael Jackson
Tonight I Celebrate My Love for You	Roberta Flack and Peabo Bryson
Always and Forever	Heatwave
We've Only Just Begun	Johnny Mathis
Truly	Lionel Richie
Here and Now	Luther Vandross

Recording Artists List For The Participants

Stevie Wonder

The Commodores

Roberta Flack

Sam Cooke

Roberta Flack and Donny Hathaway

Guy

Gladys Knight and the Pips

Pattie LaBelle and the Blue Belles

Stevie Wonder

Al Jarreau

Anita Baker

O'Jays

Jeffrey Osborne

Smokey Robinson

Diana Ross and Lionel Richie

Percy Sledge

Surface

BeBe and CeCe Winans

Larry Graham

Michael Jackson

Roberta Flack and Peabo Bryson

Heatwave

Johnny Mathis

Lionel Richie

Luther Vandross

Sistah To Sistah
A Jar of Advice for
a Happy Marriage

Before this activity, take a jar with a lid and decorate it with an Afrocentric flavor. Some ideas: Take a kente ribbon and make a beautiful bow around the top of the jar. Hot-glue different Afrocentric fabrics all over the jar. Use your imagination.

Distribute a form like the one shown below.

Sistah to Sistah

_____

_____

_____

Ask the guests to write neatly on the paper, in two sentences or fewer, their advice for a happy marriage. Once completed, ask everyone to share her advice with the entire group. Once everyone has completed the form, collect the papers, place them in the decorative jar, and present it to the bride-to-be. Encourage her to pick a piece of advice from the jar several times a week to read. The advice lives on.

Honey Call

In this game the participants are to list as many names as possible within five minutes to call their significant others. You cannot use their real names. The person with the most names wins the game. To make this really fun and exciting, ask the participants to share their lists with the group.

Some examples are:

Boo	Bear	Baby
Poo	Snookums	Darling
Pumpkin	Honey	Daddy
Chocolate Bear	Sugar	Big Daddy
Chunk	Pookie	Boopie

Soul Food Delights

Participants are to form the names of as many foods as they can within ten minutes, using each letter in the group of words listed below as the first letter of each word:

Soul Food Delights

Some examples are:

Fufu	Dressing	Dirty Rice	Okra
Succotash	Ox Tails	Grits	Tripe
Hoe Cakes	Hog Maws	Steak	Gravy
Ham Hocks	Tuna Casserole	Stew	Salad
Liver	Lamb	Deer	Goat
Salom	Duck	Sasauges	Ham
Goulash	Snap Beans	Eggplant	Fish

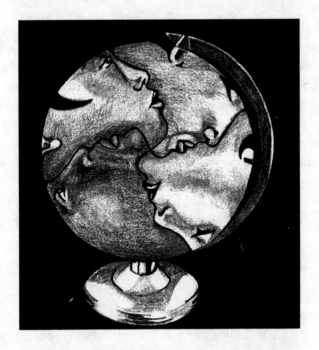

"As Your Black Love Turns"

Predict what will happen on the soap opera "As Your Black Love Turns." Each participant is to read the daily update of "As Your Black Love Turns." Then she is to predict what will happen in the next scene by filling in the blanks. She will select her answers from a variety of African-American movie titles listed on the next page. The participant with the most correct answers wins the game.

Daily update of "As Your Black Love Turns"

Yesterday, Alexia, who is a big, beautiful sistah that has it going on, was cruising down Rodeo Drive in her brand-new E-class Mercedes. She was on the way to have what she thought was just another candlelit dinner with her boyfriend of eight years, Charles. For the record, Charles is a hunk, muscles everywhere. Little does she know she is about to have the shock of her life. Charles is going to propose marriage and present her with an eight-carat marquise diamond ring, a carat for each year of their courtship. Charles has some additional news he has just found out that he must tell Alexia as soon as possible. He has been offered a job in Chicago as the Chief of Police; this is a long way from his current residence in New Orleans, La. He knows Alexia is a very successful sistah who has an income of $567,000 annually.

What will Alexia do?

Will she leave her career and move to Chicago to be with the man she loves? (Oohhhh)

Or will they have a commutable relationship? (Eeeeeeee)

What will the sistah do?

Predict what will happen in the next scene of "As Your Black Love Turns." Fill in the blank with the title from the movie list on page 48.

Well, it's <u>Friday</u>, <u>48 Hrs</u> after Charles's proposal. Alexia happily said "yes," but as the days pass she begins to think about leaving her career of fifteen years, and the fact she worked her way up from a position with a starting pay of $80,000 to $567,000. She has been blessed with promotion after promotion after promotion. Later in the day, she travels to the <u>Car Wash</u> to get her Mercedes cleaned, since a puddle of mud had been splashed on her car. As she sits in the lobby, she reflects on their relationship and how they fell in love.

It was at church, and she was wearing her favorite dress

that was The Color Purple. She needed prayer because she was Waiting to Exhale from a bad relationship with her ex-love LaJarous, who was a VIP member of The Players Club. She was thinking about How Stella Got Her Groove Back, because she wanted hers back, too. The only problem was she didn't want to have a Boomerang effect with another failed relationship. Suffering from the Love Jones, she became extremely depressed. Since she was in her own world, reflecting on the past, she missed the message the pastor was delivering. You better shake it if you're gonna make it. After the service, Deacon Charles—a 6' 5", dark chocolate, handsome man who was not wearing a wedding ring—greeted her. He said, "Hello, my sistah" with his deep voice. "Are you from around here?" She stated, "Yes, but I was born in a plantation house on Eve's Bayou." He invited her back to church; she came again and again and eight months later she joined the church. A year later, their courtship began. Charles definitely was a change from the men she had dealt with in the past; he wasn't a Nutty Professor, or a man who loves a House Party, or a man who was a Menace II Society. Charles would never do anything to make her want to Set It Off and make the man realize there is A Thin Line Between Love and Hate. Six years later, Charles is a pastor, and Alexia hopes one day to become The Preacher's Wife.

She never would have imagined Charles would be offered a job so far away. Despite the fact of making half a million dollars a year, she did the right thing, followed her heart, and married the man of her dreams. The ceremony took place at the courthouse, and immediately they moved to Chicago. Charles surprised her with a beautiful eight-bedroom house that was nestled on four acres that he called Alexia Estates. Writing had been Alexia's hobby, but she never had the time to do it. It's three years later; Alexia is now the author of three successful books. All of a sudden she begins to become ill. She goes to the doctor to find out she is three months pregnant.

Stay tuned for Charles's reaction on the next episode of "As Your Black Love Turns."

Fill in the blanks from the previous page with the appropriate title from the list below

Poetic Justice	Friday
Soul Food	Love Jones
House Party	Major Payne
Shaft	Set It Off
The Color Purple	Car Wash
New Jack City	Waiting to Exhale
Boomerang	Deep Cover
Nutty Professor	The Players Club
The Preacher's Wife	Eve's Bayou
Jungle Fever	48 Hrs.

A Thin Line Between Love and Hate
How Stella Got Her Groove Back
Menace II Society

PUT SOUL IN YOUR BRIDAL SHOWER

Notes

Bridal Shower Enhancements

Sample Bridal Shower Outlines

On the next few pages there are samples of bridal shower program outlines.

Theme Shower

Soul Food Recipe shower

Musical prelude as guests arrive

Welcome by hostess / hostesses

Hello, Girlfriends

Soul Food Scrabble

Sentimental Sistah Game

What Ya Cookin', My Sistah?

Award prizes to winners of Soul
Food Scrabble and
What Ya Cookin', My Sistah?

Bride-to-be opens gifts

Comments

Refreshments

Socializing

Theme Shower

Afrocentric Shower

Musical prelude as guests arrive

Welcome by hostess / hostesses

Hello, Girlfriends

Kwanzaa Word Game

Sentimental Sistah Game

Afro Wedding Trivia

Award prizes to winners of Kwanzaa Word Game
and Afro Wedding Trivia

Bride-to-be opens gifts

Comments

Refreshments

Socializing

Theme Shower

No *specific theme selected*

Musical prelude as guests arrive

Welcome by hostess / hostesses

Games

Hello, Girlfriends

My Pocketbook

Sentimental Sistah Game

Beauty Shop Time

Award prizes to winners of My Pocketbook
and Beauty Shop Time

Bride-to-be opens gifts

Comments

Refreshments

Socializing

Family Roots Gift Record Example

Name	Gift	Significance Summary	Sent Thank-You Note
My Mother	Grandma Rachel's Birthstone Ring	This ring was Grandma's mother's ring.	Yes
Aunt Sarah	Pearl Earrings	Aunt Sarah wore them when she got married.	Yes

Shower Gift Record Example

Theme	Soul Food Recipes
Hostess	Tonya Smith
Date	June 5
Place	Home

Guest	Gift	Sent Thank-You Note
Mary Jones	Crystal Candleholder	Yes
Michelle Ross	Lingerie	Yes

Graduation Ceremony

You can enhance the shower by having a ceremony celebrating the bride-to-be's graduation from bachelorette to married woman. This is a fun activity.

The hostess will serve as the commencement exercise facilitator.

Sistahs, we are gathered here today this _____ day of _____ to witness the commencement exercise of _____ from SGU (Sistah-Girl University), Bachelorette School of the Arts, to Being a Wife. The dean of wifehood wants you to know that you are now ready to be joined in Holy Matrimony. By the power vested in me in the county of _____ I now pronounce you a graduate and a candidate for marriage. Please come forward.

If you have computer savvy, then create a certificate like the one shown below and present it to the bride-to-be.

SISTAH GIRL UNIVERSITY
Bachelorette School of the Arts
Honorary Degree
READY TO BE A WIFE
Tonya D. Evans
JANUARY 2, 2001

Shopping List

Culinary Suggestions

Here are a few culinary suggestions listed by theme shower.

Soul Food Recipe Shower
Macaroni and cheese, collard greens,
fried chicken, corn bread, sweet potato pie

Family Roots Shower
Baked chicken, cabbage, dirty rice,
corn bread, peach cobbler

Afrocentric Shower
Yatakelt W'et (spicy mixed vegetable stew)

Inspirational Shower
Finger sandwiches, nuts, mints, crab salad,
crackers, Swedish meatballs, brownies

Lingerie Shower
Fruit tray, cheese tray, tuna noodle casserole,
crackers, cookies

Smell Good Shower
Smothered turkey, rice, mustard greens,
corn bread, candied yams

Black Art Shower
Chicken wings, tuna salad, fruit and vegetable
tray, Swedish meatballs, crackers, chocolate
covered strawberries

Designer Shower
Caviar, crackers, cheese tray, olives, ham swirls,
turkey swirls, pickle spears, potato chips, dip,
mints, little smokies, cheese balls, trussetts

Be creative in your culinary selection.

Suggested Prizes
for Game Winners

The table shown below gives prize suggestions for each game.

Game	Suggested Prize/s
Soul Food Scrabble	Certificate to a soul food restaurant
	Soul food cookbook
	Cultural coffee mug
What Ya Cookin' My Sistah?	Cultural printed mitt
	Cultural printed cooking apron
My Pocketbook	Small cultural calendar
	Cultural organizer
	Cultural printed makeup pouch
The Kwanzaa Word Game	Small Black figurines
	Book on African-American history
Afro Wedding Trivia	Cultural stationary
	Cultural printed writing utensils
Wedding Brainteasers	Subscription to a Black magazine
Beauty Shop Time	Certificate for manicure
	Certificate for pedicure
	Certificate for facial
African Proverbs	Cultural books
	Poems
Rhythm and Blues Bridal Game	Gift certificate to a music store
Honey Call	Bath and body products
"As Your Black Love Turns"	Videos featuring African-American actors

Other possible prizes include the following:

- certificate to a Black owned restaurant;
- cultural greeting cards;
- cultural day planner;
- tickets to cultural events—plays, musicals, etc.;
- cultural picture frames;
- cultural photo album;
- cultural scarf.

For those who would like to present the winner with a movie video that features African-American actors, or music videos from black artists, listed below are some titles.

Who's the Man	Harlem Nights
Bustin' Loose	Boomerang
The Nutty Professor	Coming to America
I'm Gonna Git You Sucka	Car Wash
Bebe's Kids	Vampire in Brooklyn
House Party	Petey Wheatstraw
House Party 2	The Players Club
House Party 3	Friday
Don't Play Us Cheap	Rude
Black Spring Break	Booty Call
Bulletproof	Livin' Large
Uptown Saturday Night	Major Payne
B.A.P.S.	Sister Act
Good Burger	Sister Act 2 - Back in the Habit
High School High	Stir Crazy
The Distinguished Gentleman	Mean Mother
A Thin Line Between Love and Hate	Shaft's Big Score
Talkin' Dirty After Dark	Dead Presidents
Fass Black	To Sir, With Love

A Soldier's Story
Guess Who's Coming to Dinner
Under the Cherry Moon
Rosewood
They Call Me Mister Tibbs
A Bronx Tale
The Shawshank Redemption
Miss Melody Jones
What's Love Got To Do With It?
Sweet Sweetback's Baadasssss Song
Black Sister's Revenge
Ride
Malcolm X: Death Of A Prophet
Bill Bellamy: Booty Call
Deep Cover
Boiling Point
Demolition Man
The Mack
Three the Hard Way
Black Mama, White Mama
Set It Off
Cotton Comes to Harlem
Coffy
Truck Turner
Squeeze
Lethal Weapon
Lethal Weapon 2
Lethal Weapon 3
One Down Two to Go
Juice
The Black Godfather
Philadelphia
Heaven is a Playground

Penitentiary
Penitentiary 2
Sparkle
A Time to Kill
The Bodyguard
Sweet Perfection
Blue Chips
Kiss the Girls
School Daze
Killpoint
Uncle Tom's Cabin
Phat Beach
Woo
Running Scared
New Jack City
Murder at 1600
Passenger 57
Super Fly
Foxy Brown
Friday Foster
Posse
Bucktown
Disco Godfather
Black Caesar
Dolemite
Joshua
Above the Rim
The Human Tornado
Hell Up in Harlem
Mr. Mean
Cleopatra Jones
Mo' Better Blues
Carlito's Way

PUT SOUL IN YOUR BRIDAL SHOWER

Donnie Brasco
Soul Survivor
Miss Evers' Boys
Greased Lightning
Imitation of Life
Love Jones
The Mighty Quinn
The Color Purple
Out Of Sync
Pops Staples – Live In Concert
Scarface
Menace II Society
Casino
Shaft In Africa
G.I. Bro
Black Cobra
Black Cobra 2
New Jersey Drive
Take Another Hard Ride
Big Doll House
Women in Cages
Switch Back
El Condor
Vengeance of the Black 6
Independence Day
Jo Jo Dancer, Your Life Is Calling
Purple Rain
Buck and the Preacher
Waiting to Exhale
The Education of Sonny Carson
South Bronx Heroes
Seven
Boyz 'N' the Hood

Jungle Fever
TAR
Hoover Park
Crooklyn
Soul Food
The Temptations
Shaft
Jackie Brown
A Woman Called Moses
Dead Homiez
Good Fellas
Super Fly T.N.T.
The Last Boy Scout
48 Hrs.
Black King Pin
Hit!
Trespass
The Arena
King of New York
The Big Bird Cage
Black Force
Black Force 2
Deadly Drifter
U.S. Marshals
Fresh
Money Train
South Central
Ghost
Black Like Me
Poetic Justice
Losing Isaiah
Shaka Zulu
Higher Learning

A Century of Black Cinema
Billy Blanks - Tae Boxing Workouts
A Hero Ain't Nothin' But A Sandwich
Cleopatra Jones and the Casino of Gold
How Stella Got Her Groove Back
Shirley Caesar - He Will Come (Live)
Slim and the Supreme Angels - Stay Under the Blood
Slim and The Supreme Angels - Nobody But You
Dr. Martin Luther King, Jr.: A Historical Perspective
Douglas Miller - Live in Houston
T.D. Jakes - Woman, Thou Art Loosed!

Soul Food Cookbook Resource

There are several great cookbooks that may serve as a resource in cooking a soul food meal for the shower. Listed below are a few.

LaBelle Cuisine: Recipes to Sing About
by Patti LaBelle and Laura B. Randolph (Contributor)

The Healthy Soul Food Cookbook: How to Cut the Fat but Keep the Flavor
by Wilbert Jones

Sylvia's Soul Food: Recipes from Harlem's World-Famous Restaurant
by Sylvia Woods and Christopher Styler (Contributor)

Soul Food: Recipes & Reflections from African-American Churches
by Joyce White

101 Delicious Soul Food Dessert Recipes
by Wilbert Jones

The African-American Heritage Cookbook: Traditional Recipes and Fond Remembrances from Alabama's Renowned Tuskegee Institute
by Carolyn Quick Tillery

Down-Home Wholesome: 300 Low-Fat Recipes from a New Soul Kitchen
by Danella Carter

Low-Fat Soul
by Jonell Nash

The African-American Kitchen: Cooking from Our Heritage
by Angela Shelf Medearis

The Ebony Cookbook: A Date With a Dish
by Freda De Knight

Ideas for Entertaining from the African-American Kitchen: Recipes and Traditions for Holidays Throughout the Year
By Angela Shelf Medearis

Kwanzaa: An African-American Celebration of Culture and Cooking
by Eric V. Copage

Mother Africa's Table: A Collection of West African and African-American Recipes and Cultural Traditions
By The National Council of Negro Women, Cassandra Hughes Webster

The New Soul Food Cookbook for People With Diabetes
by Fabiola Demps Gaines

Rapper's Delight: African-American Cookin' With Soul
by Al Pereira

Ruby's Low-Fat Soul Food Cookbook
by Ruby Banks-Payne

Soul and Spice: African Cooking in the Americas
by Heidi Haughy Cusick

Soul Food: Classic Cuisine from the Deep South
by Sheila Ferguson

A Taste of Heritage: The New African-American Cuisine
by Joe Randall

The African Heritage Cookbook
by Helen Mendes

Soul to Soul: A Soul Food Vegetarian Cookbook
by Mary Keyes Burgess

A Traveler's Collection of Black Cooking
byYvonne M. Jenkins

Notes

PUT SOUL IN YOUR BRIDAL SHOWER

Author's Notes

Author Tonya D. Evans may be new on the literary scene, but she is an up and rising star writing her way to becoming an acclaimed author, having written the first bridal shower book tailored to the African-American culture.

Tonya's books are written with an ethnic-based theme that is reflective of its diversity and cultural heritage.

She is an ordinary sistah with an extraordinary vision. Tonya says, *Girlfriends, make your dreams a reality, pursue them, believe in them, and most importantly, have faith in yourself.*

Faith + your vision + action = your goal

Visit Tonya's website at www.tonyadevans.com